T0082452

A
Woman's
Battles and
Transformations

Édouard Louis

TRANSLATED FROM THE FRENCH BY

TASH AW

FARRAR, STRAUS AND GIROUX

NEW YORK

Farrar, Straus and Giroux
120 Broadway, New York 10271

Library of Congress Control Number: 2022938694
ISBN: 978-0-374-60674-9

Designed by Abby Kagan

Our books may be purchased in bulk for promotional, educational, or
business use. Please contact your local bookseller or the Macmillan
Corporate and Premium Sales Department at 1-800-221-7945,
extension 5442, or by email at
MacmillanSpecialMarkets@macmillan.com.

www.fsgbooks.com
www.twitter.com/fsgbooks • www.facebook.com/fsgbooks

1 3 5 7 9 10 8 6 4 2

A Woman's Battles and Transformations

I

Everything started with a photo. I didn't know that this image existed or that I possessed it—who gave it to me, and when?

The photo was taken by her the year she turned twenty. I imagine that she must have held the camera backward to capture her face in the lens. It was a time when cell phones didn't exist, when taking a picture of oneself wasn't a straightforward thing to do.

She is tilting her head to one side and smiling slightly, her blond hair brushed and falling in immaculate bangs around her green eyes.

It was as if she was trying to be seductive.

I can't find the words to explain, but everything about the snapshot—her pose, her gaze, the movement of her hair—evokes freedom, the infinite possibilities ahead of her, and perhaps, also, happiness.

I think I'd forgotten that she had been free before my birth—even joyful?

It must have occurred to me sometimes, when I was still living with her, that she had once been young and full of dreams, but when I found the photo I hadn't thought about this for a long time—her freedom and contentment had become an abstract notion, something I vaguely knew. Nothing, or almost nothing, of what I knew of her in my childhood, through the closeness I had with her body for fifteen years, could have helped me remember all that.

Looking at this image, I felt language disappear from me. To see her free, hurtling fulsomely toward the future, made me think back to the life she shared with my father, the humiliation she endured from him, the poverty, the twenty years of her life deformed and almost destroyed by misery and masculine violence, between the ages of twenty-five and forty-five, a time when others experience life, freedom, travel, learning about oneself.

Seeing the photo reminded me that those twenty years of devastation were not anything natural but were the result of external forces—society, masculinity, my father—and that things *could have been otherwise*.

The vision of her happiness made me feel the injustice of her destruction.

I cried when I saw this image because I was, despite myself—or perhaps, rather, along with her and sometimes against her—one of the agents of this destruction.

The day of the argument with my little brother—it was summer. I came home after an afternoon spent hanging out on the steps of the village *mairie*, and a fight broke out with my youngest brother, right in front of you. Amid the shouting and the insults, my brother said, using the most hurtful tone he could muster, Everybody in the village makes fun of you behind your back. Everyone says you're a faggot.

It wasn't so much what he said that hurt me, or the fact that I knew it was true, but that he'd said it in your presence.

I went to my room and grabbed the bottle of colored sand that stood on my chest of drawers, then returned to my little brother and shattered it on the floor in front of him. It was a trinket he'd created at school. The teacher had suggested that the kids soak grains of sand in dye and fill Coke bottles with them to make colorful ornaments; she'd asked my brother if he'd wanted to make something and he'd chosen to make one for me. It was for me that he'd taken on this burden, for me that he'd spent an entire day making this pretty thing.

When I smashed the bottle at his feet he screamed sharply and began to cry, burying his face in the sofa cushion. You came up to me, slapped me, and told me that you'd never seen such a cruel child. I already regretted what I'd done, but I hadn't been able to stop myself. I was mad at my little brother for having revealed to you something of me, of my life, of my suffering.

I didn't want you to know who I was.

Throughout the first years of my life, I was terrified that you would really know me. In middle school, whenever meetings were arranged between parents and teachers, unlike other children who had good grades, I made sure that you didn't find out about them. I hid the invitations, I burned them. When an end-of-the-year variety show with sketches, songs, and dance routines was put on in the village hall, the other kids brought their parents and families along. I did everything I could to ensure your absence. I told you that the dances and songs would be boring; I made up stories about technical problems; I didn't give you the real dates for the show. I lied to you. Later I would discover an image, so often repeated in movies and TV shows, of a child on stage, waiting for his parents to appear in the hall to admire the performance that he has worked on tirelessly during that year, just for them. I never recognized myself in that child—neither in his waiting for his parents nor in his disappointment in their absence. It was as though all my childhood had been lived basically *in reverse*.

I didn't want you to know that at school, the other kids refused to be friends with me because it was frowned upon to be close to someone thought to be a *faggot*. I didn't want you to know that several times a week, two boys waited for me in the hallway of the school library to slap me and spit on my face, to punish me for being who I was. *Is it true you're a fag?*

I didn't want you to know that at the age of nine or

ten I already knew the taste of melancholy and despair, that I was prematurely aged by these feelings, that every morning I woke up with the same questions in my head: Why was I the person I was? Why was I born with the mannerisms of a girl—mannerisms that the others identified, and rightly so, as proof of my abnormality? Why was I born with this desire for other boys instead of for girls, unlike my father and brothers? Why wasn't I someone else? Once, several years after all this, when I told you during an argument that I'd hated my childhood, you looked at me as though I was crazy and said: But you were always smiling!

How could I criticize your reaction that day when it was, in a way, a symbol of my victory, of the fact that I had succeeded, throughout my entire childhood, in keeping you ignorant of what my life was—and, ultimately, in preventing you from becoming my mother?

The first pages of this story could have been called: A Son's Struggle Not to Become a Son.

The year she wanted to take a vacation—she came into the kitchen and told us she had made up her mind.

We would be going on holiday. She recalled her childhood stays in the mountains, when doctors had sent
her to the Massif Central to treat her severe asthma. I
was with my father, watching TV next to him. She
announced: We're going to the mountains. My father
laughed. He kept watching his show and said, What
the hell is that all about?

She had met with a social worker the previous day
and learned that there were programs run by the state
for families like ours who couldn't afford to go on vacation. She began to hope.

She started by shuttling back and forth to the little
building that housed the social services office, on the
edge of the fields near the metal factory. She came back
with stacks of paper under her arms, all sorts of forms
and documents freshly photocopied, still warm from
the printer, and she was charged with an energy that I
had never before seen in her, both in her body and on
her face.

She placed the documents on the table and spread
them out to show my father, but he never looked up
from the television. He replied that it didn't interest
him, so she just stayed there, immobile. She turned to
me, but I didn't listen to her either. I don't know why.

Perhaps I was unconsciously imitating my father, or maybe I was just bored by her description of the application process.

My father continued to make fun of her, but she didn't give up. I saw her heading toward the village grocery store, often several times a day, to use the photocopier next to the checkout.

She asked my father for the administrative documents that he had sorted out and filed away the previous year, but he replied that he couldn't remember where he'd put them. He said it with a faint, cruel smile on his face.

So she waited. She waited for him to go to the café before rummaging through the chest of drawers. She didn't just open them, she pulled the trays out completely and placed them on the floor, sitting next to them and taking out the piles of paper one after the other; she made phone calls, left messages, called back when she didn't get a reply, crossed the street again, filled in yet more forms; until the day she told us that it was done, she had won. Her words smothered the noise of the TV: We're going on vacation next summer. She smiled. *(Your face suddenly became so luminous.)* My father said that he wouldn't go with us, that he was better off staying at home, *chez lui*, but nothing he said mattered to her at this stage: she looked down on him now, thanks to her victory over him.

In her files she had photos of the small mountain resort I would be going to with her, as well as photos of our lodgings, and for months before our departure she would look at them every day—in the morning, at night before going to bed, hundreds of times. The day she announced the news to us, our vacation guaranteed, she whispered to me so that my father wouldn't hear, At last I'm going to be happy.

I've been told that literature should never attempt to explain, only to capture reality, but I'm writing to explain and understand her life.

I've been told that literature should never repeat itself, but I want to write only the same story again and again, returning to it until it reveals fragments of its truth, *digging hole after hole in it until all that is hidden begins to seep out.*

I've been told that literature should never resemble a display of feelings, but I write only to allow emotions to spring forth, those sentiments that the body cannot express.

I've been told that literature should never resemble a political manifesto but already I'm sharpening each of my sentences the way I'd sharpen the blade of a knife.

Because I know now that what is called literature has been constructed against lives and bodies like my mother's. Because I know, from here on, that to write about her, and to write about her life, is to write against literature.

She was born in the suburbs of a large agglomeration in the north of France. Her mother didn't work, and her adoptive father worked in a factory. She was proud of not having been born in the countryside, unlike my father. "That's why I speak better than he does."

I'm trying to remember: her father died when she was ten, from an accident that she talked about often. She kept a letter from him of barely twenty lines that he wrote in his hospital bed, when he knew he was going to die. Once or twice a year, she would take out the letter, which she'd carefully folded and stored in a yellowed envelope, and reread it, sitting on the edge of her bed. I would watch her through the gap in the door and try to understand what she was feeling.

I have nothing else to say about her childhood, nothing other than this evocation of a working-class universe and the loss of her father.

Her mother—my grandmother—was discreet, shy, self-effacing—everything a woman was expected to be. She spoke softly, cooked and cleaned, and slipped away at the end of family meals to wash the dishes while the men continued to talk and help themselves to more wine. She was born in the 1930s and at six or seven was forced to leave her home in the north because of the bombings during the Second World War. In these circumstances she hadn't been able to learn to read as a child, though she managed to catch up later in life through her own efforts. She lived a modest existence and brought up four children, my mother and her siblings; her husband died young, but she wasn't unhappy. When I spent several days with her once during a school vacation, she talked to me about my mother: "It pains me to see my daughter suffer so much. I would never have thought I'd see your mother like this."

The story of my mother starts with a dream: she was going to be a cook. An extension, most likely, of the reality of life around her: women had always done the cooking and served others. At sixteen she enrolled in the hospitality school in her region, but a year later she had to abandon her training; she was pregnant, about to give birth to my older brother, who would swiftly become alcoholic and violent, always in court or at the police station, either because he'd beaten his wife or set fire to the bus stop or the stands at the village stadium—I'll come back to that. His father, a plumber whom my mother had met a few months earlier, asked her to keep the child. They married out of convenience and moved in together. He went to work, and at eighteen she was already a "stay-at-home mom," as she put it. Perhaps, a bit later, she might have been able to pick up where she'd left off and pursue all her youthful dreams anew, but barely two years after the birth of her first child, the doctors told her she was pregnant again, and she brought a second child into the world: my older sister. At twenty, she found herself with two kids, no degree, and a husband she already hated after just a few years with him.

He would come home drunk in the middle of the night. She wouldn't know where he had spent the evening, and they'd argue. When she spoke to me about this more than twenty years later, she explained: I was stronger than him, I wasn't going to be pushed around. But it wasn't much of a life. I was tired—tired of living in a situation where I always had to be on my guard, ready to defend myself all the time.

She hated him but stayed because of the two children. She told me that she didn't want them to grow up fatherless, that she didn't want to be "responsible." Whenever she told her story she would always add: Leave him? Sure, I wanted to, but where would I go?

And yet after two or three more years with him she could no longer bear it. She'd figured out that he was sleeping with other women, that he was lying to her. He was drinking more and more. Some days—like his son years later, my older brother, these two lives repeating identically—he would wake up at seven or eight in the morning to go to work, already drunk even before he started drinking, the alcohol no longer draining from his body. So she left.

She moved in with her sister, who lived in public housing in a high-rise on the outskirts of a small industrial town, near a jumbled mass of supermarkets and huge garden centers.

She was twenty-three, with two kids, nowhere to

live, no work, no driver's license, no relatives who could help her. The only dream left, the only dream still possible for someone like her, was to rewind, to Go Back in Time. This was barely a few years after she had photographed her self-portrait.

Why do I feel as though I'm writing a sad story, when my aim was to tell the story of a liberation?

2000, or maybe 2001—memories of voices in the night; an evening when she had drunk too much. It almost never happened. In the village the roles were clearly defined: the men drank and the women tried to prevent their husbands from drinking. But some evenings she forgot all about the rules. She wanted to enjoy herself, and when my father went to buy his pastis, she would ask him to buy her a bottle of lychee liqueur, a drink called Soho. She would get drunk quickly because she wasn't used to it, and once she was in the grip of the alcohol, the same scene always unfolded: she would go to the large wooden chest where the DVD player sat and slide a disc into it, the only one she owned, a compilation by the Scorpions.

She, who otherwise never listened to music, would start singing and whistling. It's the song of my youth, she would smile.

I didn't understand why, but I hated seeing her happy, I hated the smile on her face, her sudden nostalgia, her solace.

This scene happened, in almost exactly the same way, four or five times during my childhood.

One night, at around one in the morning, I was sleeping in the bedroom next to the living room, where she was partying with my father and the neighbors, and the song started, waking me up. I got up, eyes still half-closed, my mouth dry, and went into the room where my mother and the others were. I saw the calm on her face and screamed: Stop playing this song! But this time she didn't ignore me as she had all the other times. Her eyes filled with tears of anger, she turned off the music and shouted: For fuck's sake, none of you will ever let me be happy even just once in my shitty life! Why the hell am I not allowed to be happy?

All the adults fell silent. Even my father didn't know what to do. I felt a chill run through me but I didn't apologize. I went back to my room and lay down on the bed.

I'd gotten so used to seeing her unhappy at home that the joy on her face seemed scandalous to me, a deceit, a lie that had to be exposed as soon as possible.

I'd gotten so used to seeing her unhappy at home that the joy on her face seemed scandalous to me, a deceit, a lie that had to be exposed as soon as possible.

Peeling wallpaper, the smell of food frying, children's toys scattered across the plasticky floor: life in her sister's apartment. Cigarette between her fingers, she told me: "Of course I loved your brother and your sister, and I always will, but I'll admit, when I was in that situation after having left my first husband and living in my sister's apartment, I said to myself, Why did I have two children? You can imagine how ashamed I was to think like that, but I did, all the time: Why did I have two children?"

A few months later she met my father. The only way out for her was to find another man. She fell in love, they moved in together, they had a child (me), and she felt good with him because he was *different*. But very quickly he became someone else—which is to say, he became *just like all the others*.

Often he refused to speak to her for several days at a time, for no reason. If anyone tried to say something, he'd get mad.

She shrugged; her life had become one infinite shrug: "I don't know why your dad is such a lunatic but with him, frankly, we can never tell if it's going to rain or shine."

She had only been with him for a few years but already she spoke of their relationship in the past tense: *At the beginning he took me to the beach on Sundays, we went shopping—he wasn't like he is now. He invited friends to go dancing. He wore cologne, and back then it wasn't like it is now—men didn't wear cologne, it just wasn't done. But your father did. He was different. He smelled so nice.*

He didn't want her to wear makeup, even though she desperately wanted to; he expected her to do the cooking and cleaning for the entire family; he didn't want her to get her driver's license, or at least dissuaded her from doing so; and above all, after disappearing for hours, he came home late in the evening or in the dead of night, his entire body soaked in alcohol. "It's a word that I don't use often, but now I think I can say it: your father is an alcoholic."

One day, at a village fête organized by the local soccer club, in front of the gathering of several dozen people, my father shouted to her, "Hey, you fat cow, come over here." I saw everyone's face contort with laughter. She asked me to go home with her. Back at the house, sitting on the sofa, she cried. I was eight years old, and it was the first time I saw her cry. Sobbing, she said, I don't know why your father feels the need to humiliate me like that.

She was humiliated, but she had no choice, or she felt she had none—the boundary between the two is difficult to discern—and she stayed with him for twenty years.

She did not fulfill her dreams. She couldn't fix what she saw as the succession of accidents that made up her life. She didn't find a way to travel back in time.

Am I the victim of an illusion? Is it because both she and I have distanced ourselves from this violence that I no longer see her past as a succession of tragedies and deprivations? I know that she has never accepted her fate. When she spoke about her culinary training, interrupted by her first pregnancy, she would say that she could have gone far in her studies if she hadn't had my brother. "All my teachers said I was very intelligent, especially in geography." When I asked her about her ancestors, she always claimed that she came from the extinguished line of a great French aristocratic family.

She was certain that she deserved another life, one that existed somewhere else, abstractly, in a virtual world that could so easily have been hers, and that her life in the real world was nothing but an accident.

One day, in front of the entire family, I told everyone that I would have loved it if Miss Berthe, my middle school history teacher, were my mother. I must have been eleven. My older brother, who was eating next to me, was startled: You mustn't say things like that, it's bad!

Before this, I didn't know that it was bad to wish for another mother.

Often, when she was lighting a cigarette, she would say: It's because of you all that I smoke. With such stressful kids, I'm forced to.

Another day, she walked past the schoolyard where I was playing with Cindy, a girl from the village. Cindy

asked, Is that your mother? No, I replied, I don't know
who that woman is.

**So she was living with this man she no longer loved
very much—my father.** He worked in the factory
during the day, he came home in the evening, she
served the meal.

Peter Handke summarizes his mother's daily rou-
tine in 1920s Austria: "Setting the table, clearing the
table: 'Has everybody been served?' Open the curtains,
draw the curtains; turn the light on, turn the light out;
'Why do you always leave the light on in the bath-
room?'; folding, unfolding; emptying, filling; plugging
in, unplugging. 'Well, that does it for today.'"

My mother lived thousands of kilometers from
Austria, her life unfolded more than half a century
later, her material conditions were different, and yet
her life was almost identical, right down to the expressions she used.

In the morning, when I wasn't at school, I'd see her
leave to do the grocery shopping, come home, cook the
midday meal, serve it, clear the table, wash the dishes,
clean the house, do the ironing, make the children's

beds, prepare dinner in the afternoon, wait for my father, serve us the meal, clear the table, do the dishes.

The same actions, repeated, this daily template cycling virtually every day without exception, except when she asked for a bit of help from me or my sister to do the dishes.

Another question: can I truly understand her life if it is specifically distinguished by being a woman's life—if I am constructed, perceived, and defined by the world around me as a man?

In the evening, after finishing at the factory, my father went to the café with the men he called his *copains*, his buddies. They often took their sons with them, but my father, ashamed of me and my feminine mannerisms, the mannerisms that set me apart from the others at school, never took me. I stayed at home with my mother and older sister, and it was with them that I grew up.

What is a man? Virility, power, camaraderie with other boys? I never had any of that. The absence of the risk of sexual assault? I was never protected from that.

In the same way that Monique Wittig maintains that lesbians are not women, that they escape from the constraints of that identity, the person that I am was never a man, and it is this blurring of real life that draws me close to her. It is perhaps here, in this netherland of my being, that I can attempt to understand who she is and what she lived through.

Since her life was stripped of all interest, nothing could happen unless it involved my father. She no longer had a story of her own; her story could only be, ultimately, his story. One morning, the factory called to tell us that a heavy weight had fallen and crushed my father's back while he was working. The doctors warned my mother that he would be paralyzed for several years. He would no longer receive a salary, only some benefits paid by the state as compensation. Both he and my mother went immediately from being poor to being destitute, and in order to earn some money she had to work as a home health aide, washing elderly people in the village, a job that exhausted her and that she hated.

Worst of all, my father now stayed at home all day and my mother felt suffocated. "At least he used to go to work before, and I had my days to myself."

My father was suffering—the pain refused to go

away. And like most people who suffer, he wanted to make others suffer with him. He became more aggressive toward my mother, called her hurtful names in front of others: "fat slob," "fatso," "fat cow."

And she was forced to be unkind in order to defend herself: "He could at least get off his ass and try to find work. I'm sure he's laying it on when he says it hurts."

She would tell me stories about the family or about the neighbors, but I'd never listen. I'd complain: Stop talking so much! I couldn't see that she spoke to ease the boredom, the precise duplication of hours and days that life with my father imposed upon her, and that for her, as it would be for me many years later, the telling of her life's story was the best remedy she could think of to help her bear the weight of her existence.

*S*he was certain that she deserved another life, one that existed somewhere else, abstractly, in a virtual world that could so easily have been hers, and that her life in the real world was nothing but an accident.

Unrelenting misfortune: against the backdrop of misery and tension with my father, she became pregnant. No one understood how it happened: she'd had an IUD inserted a few months earlier, to avoid further pregnancies. The doctors at the hospital told her that she was expecting not one child but two—twins. Shock. She came back from the appointment saying that she would get an abortion, that she and my father couldn't afford to raise two more children. He got upset, strangely—he who'd always been disgusted by religion, who'd always associated Religion with Power just as he connected School and the State—and said to my mother, You're crazy! We're not going to kill our children! Abortion is murder.

She tried to stand her ground, but there was nothing she could do. He decided, she ceded. A few months later she went to the hospital for the delivery. She had to stay longer than the previous times because of complications. I didn't understand the financial drama she was facing due to the arrival of these two children, the fact that they tied her even closer to my father and rendered the idea of a break with him almost impossible. I was still small, and the only thing that I could think of, the only real feeling I experienced, was that I was happy because the hospital was on the outskirts of town, near a McDonald's, and that I could eat there every day because in the euphoria of the imminent birth, my father agreed to give me money. In one week, he spent the entire amount of our state benefits, which should have lasted us until the end of the month.

The time when deprivation gave her a violent urge to participate—that was the year when a traveling circus came to the village for a few days. I wanted to go and, surprisingly, she wanted to come with me. On the evening of the show, a clown said he needed a volunteer from the audience for a magic trick. All the children in the tent raised their hands; I did too. I put my hand up as high as I could; then, afraid it wasn't high enough, I got to my feet, stretching my finger upward, and said, Me, sir, me, please, please, I beg you, choose me; and so he did. From among the hundreds of children who were there, he chose me: The little one with the blond hair, what's your name?

EDDY!

Eddy what?

EDDY BELLEGUEULE!

Haha! *Prettyface?* Nice one.

That's what he said—he thought I was joking.

I'm going to call you Fly Thighs.

I smiled and went to the middle of the tent, and he did his magic trick—I can't even remember what it was. When he was done, he sent me back to the audience and asked whom I was with. My mother raised her hand. He shouted into the microphone, Well, Madame, I return Fly Thighs to you.

She was laughing on the way home, repeating the scene, *We laughed so much!*

For months afterward, she would talk about that evening. She had, for a few minutes, been part of something, participated in real life, stepped out of the narrow role imposed upon her by life with my father, and for the first time, thanks to this joy within her, I had become her son.

In the mountains, too, throughout our vacation paid for by social security, she was transformed by joy. She was always smiling, trying to establish a closeness between us that had never existed before: Let's race to that tree over there! Loser buys ice cream for the winner this evening!

She said: You see, I'm so much less stressed and so much nicer when your father isn't with me—he's the reason I'm nasty.

But I'll continue: the arrival of two new children. To bring one more child into this family would have made her life much more complicated; two more were a catastrophe. There were seven people in the house—the five of us kids, and my parents.

In this configuration, even feeding ourselves became difficult. Once a week my mother would call out from the kitchen, "Put on your shoes, we're off to Pont-Remy!" I knew what this meant. A charitable association there gave out food. My mother wanted me to accompany her because she knew that having a child with her would elicit sympathy from the women who distributed the food, and on seeing me they would perhaps add an extra box of pasta or cookies.

Poverty always adheres to an operating manual that no one has to spell out: no one explained it to me, but I knew that I couldn't tell anyone in the village about these trips to the food bank. I didn't talk about it with my parents either. We would go to Pont-Remy, collect the food, and come home without saying a word about it, as if it never existed.

In this new situation, my father's aggression reached extreme levels. My mother and he actually came from different factions of the poor: everyone in her family was a factory worker—her adoptive father, her brother, her sister. My father's family was much poorer: alcoholism, mental illness, prison, unemployment. It was because of this difference that, with the arrival of the two new children, my father felt that my mother's family should have given us some money. When they didn't, my father got mad and sometimes stopped her from going to see them. She couldn't drive, and he would refuse to take her to the village where they lived.

When he'd drunk too much he'd say: "Your family are a bunch of filthy Jews, they deserve a good gassing."

My mother: "I think it's awful because you can't prevent someone from seeing her family. Why does he stop me from seeing my own mother?"

Not only was she a mother to five children, with no money and no prospects, she was a prisoner of the domestic sphere. All the doors were locked.

What could she do? She did everything she could not to suffocate completely:

Some days she would look at my younger brother and sister and she'd smile: My kids are so beautiful. I felt bad when I decided to keep them because I knew we didn't have enough money, but now I don't regret it at all. They're so beautiful.

She made fun of the way other women looked: That one, she's like a barn door: huge and flat.

She loved ready-made sayings, anything that expressed itself in a concise way: I don't have cash, my life is trash!

Poverty doesn't lead to being slovenly! Beware the sleeping wolf! Dogs that bite once bite again.

Yet even in these moments I could see that the melancholy never left your face.

II

Is it something you think about often? **One day you thought that friendship could lead you out of this life**—it was 2006; you and my father had talked to Angélique at the village fête. It wasn't about whether you two knew or didn't know Angélique, it was something else. She was in charge of the power grid in the region. She worked in an office and had studied for two or three years at university. These details alone were enough to separate her radically from a family like ours; she wasn't friends with people like us, but rather with teachers, middle managers at the factory, employees of the *mairie*, those we saw every day in the street and acknowledged but never spoke to, another caste—since everyone knows that, contrary to what you might think, the closer people are to each other physically, as they are in the countryside, the more rigid class barriers are.

It was my father who first approached her—he saw her standing alone several meters from your group and noticed that not only was she on her own, she was also crying. You two would often leave the village fêtes early, but that year you'd stayed longer than usual, and the village square was already empty when my father went up to Angélique to ask what was wrong, and to invite her to our place to have some drinks, to console her—I think that he found her attractive too, that he had been in love with her all these years, but that's not important. He always had a propensity for helping others, it's true, and you used to complain, you used to say to me that you didn't understand why my father was so mean to his own family yet so sweet and even generous to others, to strangers, always ready to help out, with *repairs*, as he used to say. I think it was because he was suffocating from life at home and because he wanted to make his family pay for being his family, for being the face of his suffering—but that isn't the story here. Angélique nodded without saying anything, and I saw the tears on her cheeks, like two bright and almost parallel lines. My father put his hand on her shoulder, and she followed us home. Once she was sitting on the sofa, she told you two what had happened, and I can remember what she said: how and why the man she loved had just left her, how at her age she was scared to live out her life alone and childless. She said all this between sobs and long-drawn breaths.

My father took her in his arms, and you talked to her. You said what people say in such situations, that everything would be all right, that she would soon forget him, that one should never count on men for anything. I watched you all from the sofa, and I don't know how to describe the state in which I found myself, this fascination and apprehension at having someone from a different background in our house, like the times when the doctor called round in the evening and our bodies changed because of his very presence—we held ourselves differently, spoke differently, afraid that a simple gesture would reveal our social inferiority.

Angélique came back to the house the next day, and the day after that. She grew closer to both of you, and immediately you felt that she would lead you toward another life, toward other habits from another world, ways of living that were freer and gentler. You were instantly happier—am I mistaken? The more she came, the more you adopted her life. She booked you appointments at the hairdresser, when for years you'd cut your own hair with kitchen scissors; she taught you different expressions that gave you greater self-confidence—you now said "Absolutely" when someone else was speaking, do you remember? She helped us discover foods we'd never known—taramosalata, hummus, foods that made us feel different and distinguished when we ate or bought them.

Your whole body changed. The sadness vanished from you.

Were you aware of the social miracle that was playing out? Of this sudden possibility of escaping yourself? I think you were. Thanks to Angélique, you felt stronger when facing my father; you had an ally now. As you hung the laundry on the line and I held the container of clothespins for you, you whispered, *I think that sometimes Angélique must get really fed up with your dad, who doesn't know how to speak or behave properly.*

I can't make a list of everything that happened thanks to her, through her. The two of you went to the supermarket to buy underwear, you went to the seaside, *just us girlfriends*, as you used to say. (I started this book wanting to tell the story of a woman, but I've realized that yours is the story of a human being who fought for the right to exist as a woman, as opposed to the nonexistence imposed upon you by your life, and by life with my father.)

During the two or three years of your friendship with Angélique, her depression never fully went away; she still cried, often; she fell in love easily. When a childhood friend of my father's—whom he hadn't seen in fifteen years because he'd become a soldier and been stationed at a barracks in the south of France—returned to the village and came to dinner, she did everything she could to seduce him. She bought new clothes and makeup, she had her nails done in the booth at the big supermarket where we went shopping on Saturday afternoons. When the love affair with this man failed, she fell in love with my older brother. He hit her, and we'd find her in the afternoon with bruises under her eyes, but still she clung to him as much as she could.

And you continued spending days and weekends out with her, laughing with her, becoming like her.

But one day everything stopped. Angélique met a man; she loved him, and he suggested they have a child together. Her melancholy, which had never left her body since your meeting at the fête, eventually dried up and she slowly began to distance herself from our family. She came over less often, her messages came less frequently, and she no longer suggested going out with you. At first you didn't understand. You said that it was odd but it must have been due to work, that there was nothing to worry about. Then you were forced to see that she no longer came to our house, that she no longer answered your calls. Once, some time after her silence began, you met her in the street coming back from the bakery, but she didn't say hello. You sighed, eyes cast downward, your face fixed: She didn't even say hello to me. I don't understand. We were friends, weren't we?

Still, you rang her again, you tried one last time, but when she finally answered she told you to leave her alone. Leave me alone, Monique.

She had ended your relationship. Did I ever tell you that I went to see her, at her place? I missed her too.

When she opened the door I felt tears welling up in my eyes, and I asked her why she'd disappeared. She explained that she could no longer stand our family, our table manners, the way my father spoke to you, the constant and obsessive presence of the TV—she couldn't take it anymore. Her depression had changed her perception of the world; she had felt welcome in our house, but now that she was in love and, she said, happy, everything that had previously been invisible to her was now unbearable.

It was as if this romantic depression, a psychological factor, had somehow rendered porous the usual laws of sociology—the fact that people from a certain milieu socialize only with those of the same milieu, and that there is virtually no possible mixing between social classes.

Now it was finished. When you spoke of her, you shrugged and said: We weren't good enough for her anyway.

You felt abandoned,

and you were,

you were alone.

III

Not so long ago, you called me. You asked if I was doing well, and after a short conversation about my younger brother and the weather, platitudes like that, you told me that you needed to earn some money for yourself, for daily life and for going out—I didn't know what you meant by that, going out. You let several seconds pass, took a breath, and continued: "That's why I need some work. And I thought I could do the cleaning for you. I'll come when you're not at home, of course—I won't disturb you. I clean the place, you leave the money on the table, I go."

I forced myself to reply, despite my surprise. What could I say? I tried, in any case; I told you that it just wasn't possible. I added that I could give you a bit of money if you needed it, but you went on, No, no,

I'm not asking for alms. What I need is work. Think about it.

When I was with you in the village as a child and I saw privileged people—the mayor, the minor gentry, the owners of the pharmacy, the grocer—I mostly hated them because I saw in them all the privileges that I didn't have access to.

I hated their bodies, their freedom, their money, their ease of movement.

If that day you asked to become my cleaning lady, does it mean that I had become one of those bodies?

Had I become one of those bodies I'd hated?

The story of our relationship began on the day of our separation. It was as if we'd reversed time, you and I, as if the separation had preceded the relationship and laid its foundations.

Everything changed during my first year in high school. I was the only person from our family to have had an education. There, at school, I was brutally confronted by a world I didn't know. The people I met, who became my friends, read books and went to the theater, sometimes even the opera. They traveled. They had ways of speaking, dressing, and thinking that were totally different from what I had known with you. I was entering the universe of those you'd always called *les bourgeois*, and immediately I wanted to be like them.

When I came back to the village those first times, I wanted to show you my new membership—that is to say, the growing divide between my life and yours. It was above all through language that I made this distinction. I was learning different words in high school, and these words became the symbols of my new life— unimportant words like *bucolic*, *fastidious*, *laborious*, *underlying*. They were words I'd never heard before. I used them with you, and you got annoyed: Enough of your minister's vocabulary! You'd say, *That* guy—ever since he went to high school he thinks he's better than us.

(And you were right. I said those words because I did think I was better than you. I'm sorry.)

All at once, any exchange between us became a conflict. When you showed me something by pointing to it and you said *Garde* instead of *Regarde*—as I had done since I was a baby, and as we had always done—I would call you on it: It's *regarde*, not *garde*. When you began a sentence with "If I would have," I'd correct you: If I *had*. The *if* doesn't go with *would have*.

I spoke in sentences that seemed exotic to you, imported directly from the world I would inhabit from now on. *It'll soon be teatime, do you know where I left my newspaper?* I gave you advice: *Why don't you get my brother and sister to listen to a bit of classical music, some Mozart or Beethoven? It's really good for the brain, you know.* You raised your eyebrows. This guy's gone completely nuts. I've raised five kids—he's not going to teach me how to bring up children.

(Often you didn't exist at all, you had disappeared from my memory. I lived my life at school as if I had never known you.)

Most people who speak about their trajectory passing from one social class to another recount the violence they experienced in the process—because of their inability to adapt, their ignorance of the codes of the world into which they were entering. I remember mostly the violence I inflicted. I wanted to use my new life as revenge against my childhood, against all the times when you and my father made me understand that I wasn't the son you had wished for.

I became a class defector out of revenge—and this violence was added to all the rest that you had already lived through.

The time she was summoned to my high school to sign some administrative papers—I said earlier that in middle school I had always succeeded in avoiding having her accompany me, for fear that she would learn how to get to know me, fear of any reconciliation with her, however minor. I didn't want her to come to my high school either, but not for the same reason; it was a new feeling I was experiencing, a feeling that drove me to invent strategies to keep her away: I didn't want the others to see her, and to see through her another person in me—my past, the poverty. I didn't want the others to know that my mother didn't look like theirs, that my mother hadn't had an education, had never traveled, didn't have clothes as fine as theirs, that she wasn't cheerful and sleek like their mothers. I had succeeded in hiding her existence, but one day the school told me I had no choice; she had to come. I went to see her in the kitchen where she was doing the crossword and told her that she had to take the train with me, all the way to school. She started out by saying as always that it wasn't possible, that she was too busy with house-work, but then, as I insisted, changed her mind.

A few days later I was with her on the little train with gray-and-blue-striped seats, heading toward the school in Amiens. It was stupid, but I was afraid of being seen by people I knew, people from my new world.

About two or three hundred meters from the place where she was to sign the papers, I said to her, Please don't put your finger up your nose while you're speak-ing, and try to speak nicely. Otherwise I'm going to be so ashamed. Everyone else's mother speaks well.

She stopped on the sidewalk and looked at me: You really are a little shit. I saw the disgust on her face.

For the rest of the day she walked alongside me in silence.

On the train home I was only a meter away from her, but I felt hundreds of kilometers from her body. She looked out the window at the endless parade of fields and forests. Amid the silence she asked, So, not too ashamed of me then?

When I was a child, we felt ashamed together—of our house, of our poverty. Now I was ashamed of you, against you.

Our shame had parted ways.

Life continued, and for her it continued to resemble a fight against life. My youngest brother and sister were fourteen and already beginning to drift away from school, no longer going to class, their grades in every subject collapsing. She knew that without qualifications their lives would turn out like hers, and she was in despair. "I keep pushing them and telling them to go to school, but they don't want to. Yesterday I asked them, Do you want to be counting your pennies for the rest of your lives, just like me? But they get mad when I say that. What can I do?"

My younger brother was sinking into a radically

contemporary kind of life that she wasn't familiar with, and for which she had neither language nor remedy. He woke up at ten and turned on his gaming console. He played all day until late into the night. He came downstairs only once a day to fetch some food from the kitchen. He didn't eat with the rest of the family; he took his plate back up to his room. He put on weight, he didn't have friends, his face became shrouded with grayish shades.

As for my older brother, he was vanishing into his problems with alcohol. He hit the woman he lived with, as he had done with Angélique, and she would call my mother in the middle of the night to warn her that she would press charges the next time it happened.

When my mother spoke about it to me, she clung with all her strength to her denial of the evidence. "I saw your older brother yesterday, and this time I think it'll be fine. He promised me he's going to stop drinking." But then he would start again with the drinking and the violence, and she too would start again, start lying to herself again, in some infernal cycle: "I know that this time he went too far, but he promised me. Now it's all right—he's understood, he's got it into his head, he won't drink again. I saw him, I sorted things out with him, and he swore to me that he'll never touch a drop of alcohol again."

She was desperate to deny reality, and yet I could see it—she regarded the destiny of her sons as a dreadful repetition of the mechanisms that had crushed her own life, as the unbreakable cycle of a curse.

Sometimes she said, laughing: Monica Bellucci is the Italian translation of Monique Bellegueule. Monique Bellegueule, Monica Bellucci. I am the French Monica Bellucci. She would toss her hair back as she said it, just like a movie star.

When talking about her imaginary aristocratic family, she would give details: "He was a nobleman, my great-grandfather, but one day he fell in love with the woman who sold fish at the market and his family disinherited him. He chose love over money. Really, I should have been an aristocrat. I have blue blood. It sucks."

———

When I announced to her that I was gay, she replied anxiously, Well, I just hope you're not the woman when you're in bed!

It's an anecdote that makes me laugh nowadays.

The day of the incident—I was sixteen, and I tried to come back to your house as little as possible during the school year; I stayed with friends in Amiens. But in the summer I returned for four weeks, sometimes longer, to work as a group leader with the children at the village rec center.

At around ten in the morning that day, I was choreographing some dances with a group of girls when all of a sudden I was struck by a violent pain in the pit of my stomach. A little girl came up to me and put her arms around me, but the mere touch of her hands hurt me. I couldn't bear it any longer; I sat on the floor, winded. The pain had come on so swiftly, there had been no hint as to what might have been happening. The director of the center came and knelt down next to me. She told me to go home and call a doctor—maybe she offered to call one for me and I refused, I can't remember.

I walked the three or four hundred meters back to the house; my stomach was hurting more and more; once I was home, on the sofa, I realized that my hair was wet, my back too; I was sweating.

You were watching TV in the same room. You were the only one at home, and I told you I wasn't well. I asked you to call an emergency doctor or an ambulance but you didn't want to. You took a drag of your cigarette and replied that it was nothing.

I saw what was happening: you thought I was exaggerating the pain because I was behaving like city folk, the people I had wanted to be like ever since I started at the high school in Amiens, privileged people. In our world, medicine and relationships with doctors had always been considered a way for *les bourgeois* to feel important by taking meticulous and extreme care of themselves. Essentially, I think you saw this scene as an extension of all the others since the beginning of our estrangement; as my way of showing a class difference, of attacking you. (And how could I reproach you for it, since it's true, I was waging a war against you?).

But the pain didn't subside; in the end, I got up from the sofa and told you I was going to see the doctor. I went to the door and opened it, and you let me leave without saying a word to me, the cigarette still firmly between your fingers. As soon as I reached the doctor's, he examined me and told me that my appendix was about to explode.

I spent two weeks in the hospital. My appendix had become infected, and the infection had spread throughout my body. The nurses told me: A few more hours and you could have died.

The distance in social class had so contaminated our relationship that you saw me only as an instrument of class aggression, and this situation had nearly killed me.

And yet the divide continued to deepen, inexorably. After high school I enrolled at the university in the same city, Amiens, and our mutual incomprehension reached new levels.

There are separations more brutal than family breakups: she and I didn't argue any more than at all the other times; there wasn't any shouting or slamming of doors. It was simply that we could no longer find anything to say to each other. The few times I spoke to her on the phone I concluded that her life was already fixed forever, in advance: her trips to the village grocery store, the preparing of meals, her children who were merely reproducing her life, the boredom of living in the countryside, my father's nastiness toward her. She was barely forty, but nothing more could happen. And it was precisely at this moment, when I was formulating these ideas, that everything changed.

IV

One night, the year after my near-death, another call. Her voice rang out in the darkness around me: "At last. I've done it." I had been reading on the sofa and was surprised to see her number show on my screen. She was speaking quickly, her voice breathless with the exhilaration of a teenager. She was my mother, but suddenly she was younger than I was.

I understood immediately what she was talking about, and I replied with the same excitement: "Tell me everything! How did it happen?" She caught her breath: "As usual, he didn't come home—you know what he's like. Anyway, he'd been gone since I don't know when, and I'd done the cooking and was waiting for him. But then I thought: It's over. I'm not waiting any longer. I'll never wait for him again. I'm fed up with waiting."

(I was proud of you. Did I tell you?)

She continued, "So I put all his things in trash bags and threw them out on the sidewalk. Just like that. I couldn't stop myself. He came back and tried to open the door, but I'd locked everything. He banged on the walls and windows, and shouted. I know him all too well—I think he knew exactly what was happening. I told him through the door never to come back. He asked, Never? And I repeated, Never again. He cried, but I said to myself, Don't you give in. Don't you give in. No more giving in."

She spoke as if she were telling me about the unfolding of an escape or a burglary that the two of us had worked out together, patiently, secretly, for months and years.

From the time I stopped living with her, I saw only violence in her life. In my new world, women were not treated the way my mother was and had been, or as the other women in the village were. I never saw a man insult his wife in public in Amiens. I never saw faces swollen like my sister's after her arguments with the man who lived with her, or like Angélique's after her arguments with my brother. I knew no one in high school or at university who could say what I could say: My sister gets beaten up by the man she lives with, and my brother beats up the woman he lives with.

(Of course violence against women existed in Amiens too, but not as much, and when it happened, not in such a systematic manner.)

It was as though, through my contact with the bodies of the bourgeoisie of Amiens, I was starting to see the world of my childhood after the fact, a posteriori, through the distance between these worlds. Through my detachment from her, I had learned to *see* the violence, and I saw it everywhere.

I thought she should speed up. When I spoke to my mother—the few times I did after my departure from the village—I encouraged her to leave my father. I told her she couldn't ruin her life by staying with a man who made her unhappy and who humiliated her. She would reply, "I'm going to do it, I want to do it, but for the moment it's too difficult, what with your brother and sister." *(I didn't realize that it was true. I didn't see the difficulties you faced.)* I pressed her, repeated that she shouldn't wait, that what was at stake was her freedom, that she could see to my brother and sister later, and she would reply, "Yes, soon. You'll see, soon."

So when she called me the night she finally did it, she concluded her story in a triumphal and defiant voice: "You see, I told you I'd do it. I'd already done it once with my first husband, so I could do it a second time. I knew I could do it a second time."

Our distance had brought us closer together.

It's strange: We both started our lives as History's losers—she the woman, I the dissident, monstrous child. But as in a mathematical equation, a perfectly symmetrical inversion, the losers of the world we shared became the winners, and the winners the losers. After the breakup, my father's health declined. He was alone, even poorer than when he lived with her. He, who had held all the power over us in the first part of his life, now found himself destitute of everything; the sadness would never again leave his face. Everything that had been his strength became his weakness: the alcohol he had consumed all his life had ruined his body; his lifelong refusal to seek medical care—he'd said that medication was only fit for women—had weakened his organs; the years of work in the factory and later as a street sweeper—he'd said that it was up to the man to support the family—had broken his back.

As for my mother, she started ringing me several times a month. "If you could see how free I am now! You wouldn't recognize me."

The time she received a multicolored letter in the mail—I was twelve. Inside the envelope was a letter addressed directly to her, complete with her first name: DEAR MONIQUE, YOU'VE BEEN SELECTED FOR A SPECIAL DRAWING. REPLY TO THIS LETTER AND YOU MAY WIN THE INCREDIBLE SUM OF 100,000 EUROS. We looked at each other, eyes wide. She pursed her lips and said, It seems real, doesn't it? If it was a scam, they wouldn't have used my real name. They couldn't have known it. I said I agreed with her, was convinced by her reasoning, and I encouraged her to respond. As she filled in the form beside me, I felt the adrenaline rush through both of us. She filled in the boxes carefully—last name, first name, address—and I saw her deliberately adding loops at the tops of the L's and under the J's, trying to produce the most beautiful and precise handwriting possible. Between each box she'd lift her head and whisper, Imagine if we won the hundred grand! She made me promise not to say anything to my father— she knew he'd be angry if he found out about it. I swore to her that I wouldn't tell him; I was happy to be able to hide something from him with her consent, as if I were entering the adult world.

A few days later I collected the mail that had just arrived, and I spotted a new colorful envelope in the pile. I ran toward her, shouting, Oh my god Oh my god Oh my god Oh my god Oh my god. She opened the letter, her fingers trembling. The letter read: YOU'RE CLOSER THAN EVER TO THE 100,000 EU-ROS, MONIQUE! Send a check for 5 euros to have your name entered in the drawing twice, thereby multiplying your chances of WINNING. She bit her lower lip. It's worth it, don't you think? If we win a hundred thousand it'll be worth losing five. I nodded like a madman, Yes, yes, do it. She sent the check, and a few days later we received a new letter asking us for a new check for a chance to win a giant high-definition flat-screen TV WHILE AWAITING THE GRAND PRIZE DRAWING. We sent the check, and then another, and then another again. With each new letter I felt my heart rate quicken, but after the fourth or fifth letter asking again for a check, she understood, and I understood with her, that it had all been a scam. She sighed, Well I think we've been cheated. Or else we read it wrong, and *they* were the ones asking *us* for a hundred thousand euros in checks of five. For several days afterward I dreamed of what our life could have been like with the hundred thousand euros, and then I thought no more of it.

A hypothesis: I think that if it hadn't been for our reconciliation over these last years—a coming together that started with our drifting apart—I wouldn't have remembered this story. It is because our relationship has changed that I can now see our past with a certain benevolence, or rather, revive these fragments of tenderness amid the chaos of the past.

Our reconciliation has not only changed her future, it has also transformed our past.

She looked for a job. She had to make up for the loss of money after the breakup with my father, so she started to work again helping old people in the village wash and dress. She insisted, "I'm not a cleaning lady, mind you, I'm a home health aide. It's almost like being a nurse."

The importance of minuscule differences, the fear of being at the bottom of the social ladder, the wish not to be part of the most socially undesirable professions—jobs whose names immediately evoke suffering and poverty: cleaning lady, cashier, trash collector, street sweeper. Some days the terror of these tiny differences morphed into anger: "These nurses, I don't know who they think they are. They're so proud of their diplomas, but I basically do the same thing as them. I do even more."

She even complained of not having enough work. This work that she'd hated when she lived with my father because it was a component of her life of suffering suddenly became an instrument of her liberation. Words and realities had changed meaning.

It had been several months since she'd left my father, and she was living with my younger brother and sister in public housing on the edge of the fields, where she had been relocated by social services. She told me, enthusiastically: There are bedrooms upstairs! Your brother and sister each have their own room.

She boasted: See how resourceful I am, I found a new place right away. Your father wouldn't have known how to do that!

How to say this without being naive or without sounding as if I'm using a dumb, ready-made expression: it was moving for me to see you happy.

As with every transformation, what followed was tied up with a new encounter. The meeting took place one evening in the village, at the house of a friend who had invited her over to celebrate her birthday. The friend's brother was there. My mother had never seen him before; he lived in Paris, where he worked as an apartment building superintendent.

He attempted to seduce my mother all evening, and she didn't try to resist—quite the opposite, she wanted an adventure and she encouraged him to keep going, though she warned him: men can't get the better of me anymore!

They saw each other again. He liked my mother's cheerful, sparkling personality, unaware that this personality had only just emerged, that it had been smothered for twenty years. He asked her to move in with him in Paris, but she refused. She wanted to get to know him properly: "I've already been tricked by two men, and it's not going to happen with a third. I love my freedom too much. Now that I have it, I'm not letting go of it."

They grew closer, and she understood that he wouldn't be like my father or her first husband: "With him, I'm the one who gives the orders. It's me who lays down the law."

In her life, love had always been a space in which one either gave or received orders, not a space where power relations were suspended.

On TV, she had heard a presenter speak of her "woman's pride," and she started using this expression to explain all her choices and decisions. In her own way, she became a political subject.

I encouraged her to abandon her role as a mother. My younger brother, who was eighteen, still lived with her; he didn't go to school, he didn't work, he continued to spend more than ten hours a day on his gaming console.

My mother sighed, "I can't take him with me to

Paris, but I don't want to leave him all alone either. I'm not like those mothers who abandon their kid."

I told her she should think of herself, that even though he was her son, he was also a man, and she couldn't let yet another man ruin her life. I was starting to understand that when a son stands before his mother, even if he is a son, he is still a man standing before a woman.

She hesitated: "Yes, but what can I do? I can't leave my kid to fend for himself." She was tempted by the call of freedom, but she still felt responsible. I pressed her: "My brother will manage. You've earned the right to be selfish now."

A year later, she moved to Paris,* where I was also living, and where I was continuing the studies I'd started in Amiens. When I went to meet her for the first time on the street where she now lived, I couldn't believe the person she had become, the person I saw before me. Nothing about her resembled the woman who had been my mother. She wore makeup, her hair was colored. She wore jewelry. A few weeks away from the village, and from what had been her life for too long, had been enough to transform her appearance radically. She saw the surprise in my eyes and— forever her own theoretician—said: "You see, I'm not

---

* She was right to do so, not just for her but for my brother too. One transformation leads to others. After she left, he found a place to stay, found friends, new interests. One day he told me, I'm transformed now—I had become a zombie.

the same! I'm a real *Parisienne* now." I smiled. "Yes, it's true. It's true, you're the queen of Paris."

She took me in her arms and kissed me on the cheek.

And then you met Catherine Deneuve. I had become a writer and was invited to watch a film shoot at which she was present. At some point, a man behind me announced a break and asked if I would like to speak with Catherine Deneuve. I said yes and followed him; when I found myself in front of her, because I was scared of speaking to her, I consciously searched for a sentence, something to say that wasn't too serious or too trite, and I thought of you, since you were someone who both admired her and had a life that couldn't have been more different from hers. I told her that you lived close to where she did, thinking that it was an amusing anecdote that would avoid the usual platitudes or small talk about politics or the news.

Catherine Deneuve raised her eyebrows; I saw that

she was surprised, and I told her about your transformation, your arrival in Paris, your life with your partner, the building superintendent. She smiled and, between two drags on her cigarette, said that she would visit you someday.

A few days later, you called me. "Guess who I've just smoked a cigarette with! Catherine Deneuve!"

I never thought she would do it. I thought she said she'd visit you merely out of politeness, to find something to say, to avoid the awkwardness of a first conversation.

You told me how Catherine Deneuve had come and stood in front of your building and had suggested having a smoke and a chat. "I was looking around discreetly while we talked because I hoped as many people as possible would see me talking with her. I wanted everyone to know that Catherine Deneuve was talking to me."

I had never heard such emotion in your voice, as if this interaction with an actor you'd admired since you were young represented and condensed all the efforts you had made in your transformation. You summed it up, brow furrowed: "I've been pushed around all my life, but now I'm in Paris and I know Catherine Deneuve."

Indeed, in Paris she started using new sentences, reflections of her new existence. *I went for a stroll in the Luxembourg Garden today. I had coffee on the terrasse at a café near my place.*

I don't know if she was fully aware that the mere possibility of saying these sentences was a revolution in itself. These were sentences that I had, on my arrival in Paris, associated with the world of intellectuals and the bourgeoisie, with the privileged, with Simone de Beauvoir's *Mémoires*—and therefore with the complete opposite of what she had been.

When I brought up the village in conversations with her, she would sigh. "Ah, the country mentality! Now that I'm in the city, I could never live in the countryside again, not as long as I live, that's for sure."

All of a sudden, happiness gave her youth. When we were living together, she had only ever mentioned her early days, almost by accident, on the three or four occasions when I'd seen her drunk; now she told me long stories of how she'd gone to nightclubs as a teenager with her girlfriends before her marriage at the age of eighteen, and how she'd met one of her best friends on the dance floor, someone who was *like me*, meaning homosexual.

I didn't understand why she had never told me about him before, when I was a child, at a time when I wanted to die because of what I was, because I felt sick and abnormal.

I listened to her telling me these new stories and thought of the woman who had been my mother during those years in the village,

When she cycled through the streets, her silhouette blurred by the fog, her body surrounded by the brick walls, surrounded by the northern gray,

When she wore her red coat, too big for her because it had belonged to my father and she couldn't afford to buy another one, the sleeves making her hands disappear, the hood hiding her face,

When she found out that the women of the village gathered in the square in front of the *mairie* and made fun of her because of her oversize coat, but she said she didn't care,

When those women and their nastiness consti-
tuted her only horizon,

When, in the afternoons, she fell asleep in front of
the TV after having done the housework, the house
completely silent, the smell of cleaning products and
of the damp floating in the air amid the silence,

When she vanished into domestic life

I am a slave to this shithole

When she punched me out of anger, and I saw that
each blow made her feel good (once or twice in my
entire childhood)

When she coughed from her cigarettes

When she shouted

When she walked

When she dreamed

When she complained that my father only gave her
household appliances, vacuum cleaners or deep-fat
fryers for her birthdays

I'm not just a maid

When I thought: I don't know her

When she crushed me

When she told me, disgusted and upset, *Can't you
be a bit normal from time to time?*

When she made me go and ask my aunt for a box
of pasta because we had nothing left to eat

When she shrugged and said, What a shitty life we have

When she laughed in spite of that

When she spoke of Angélique with tears in her eyes

When she said she'd have liked to be a lesbian so she could live without men

When she suffered

When she received court summonses for my older brother

When she repeated, again, What a shitty life we have

When she suffered

She saw the surprise in my eyes and said: "You see, I'm not the same! I'm a real Parisienne *now." I smiled. "Yes, it's true. It's true, you're the queen of Paris."*

The liberation continued. It had been six months since she inhabited this new existence. The afternoons I met her, once every month or two, she always turned up in new clothes, always smiling. They weren't quality clothes or particularly luxurious, but it didn't matter. She was happy to have become a woman who bought clothes, to be doing, as she said herself, *what other women do*: wearing makeup, taking care of herself, doing her hair.

For some people, a woman's identity is clearly an oppressive one; for her, becoming a woman had been a conquest.

One evening during this new life, I took her to the bar of a fancy hotel, a *palace* in fact, as a treat for her. I walked in with her, and we sat down next to an immense fireplace. A woman took our coats; a man with a white napkin over his arm served us. I saw that she was tense, that she was afraid of committing a faux pas. She ordered the same cocktail as I did, and she observed my gestures and posture. She copied them, no doubt thinking that I knew this world and its codes. She replied, "Yes, quite, absolutely, absolutely," to everything I said. She was playing a role. And yet— and this is what I wanted to get to—I saw, above all else, her thrill at living this moment, in this temple of luxury, stealing a life that should not have been hers. Narrowing her eyes, she said, "We've done well, both of us." After our drink I took her home, and before going up to her apartment, she said: "Can we do that again soon? I just want to enjoy myself!"

Another time, I took her to dinner at the restaurant at the top of the Montparnasse Tower for her birthday. I'd told my friends the day before that I was worried she might be intimidated by the setting, and that it might prevent her from enjoying the occasion—this had happened with my father the year before, when I'd invited him to a restaurant that specialized in grilled meat because I knew it was what he liked; when he opened the menu he refused to order the best dishes, the ones I suggested, because he was shocked by the prices. He asked for a simple *steak haché*, the cheapest item on the menu, saying over and over that he didn't want me spending too much money. I was afraid that my mother would do the same, but when the waiter gave us the menus, she chose the foie gras and the lobster, and even suggested drinking some champagne. Let's have some bubbles, shall we? She didn't want to lose this chance to live a different life.

Roland Barthes: "[Her] (admissible?) dream would be to transport into a socialist society certain *charms* [. . .] of the bourgeois art of living [. . .] What rises up against this dream is the specter of Totality, which demands that the bourgeois phenomenon be condemned *entire*, and that any leak of the Signifier be punished. (Might it not be possible to take one's pleasure in bourgeois [deformed] culture *as a kind of exoticism*?)"

During those evenings in the luxury hotel or at the top of the Montparnasse Tower, it was this exoticism that I shared with her.

———

What does it mean to change?

In what I know of her today, there are dozens of images and facts that contradict the simple story of a happy transformation. She has never traveled outside of France; she continues to buy food at low-cost supermarkets for the poor on the outskirts of Paris; she doesn't earn any money, so she still relies on the man she lives with; she can't make friends with the people in her neighborhood, the rich women on her street who look at her condescendingly. She admits: There are days when I get bored. I don't have friends here. People here aren't like us.

Is a change still a change when it is circumscribed to this extent by class violence?

And yet. And yet she is happy. She keeps telling me this. I no longer know what or how to think. Perhaps the question is not what change means, but what happiness means. I haven't found any answers, but I know that her current existence, what she has become, forces me to confront the question.

———————

Like me, she has changed her last name. She no longer wanted to be called Bellegueule, the name I inherited when I was born, and had shared with her, a heavy, lower-class name. She chose for herself a last name based on her mother's maiden name and that of her adoptive father. When she showed me her new identity card, she said, "Sounds posh, doesn't it?"

She buys romance novels from the supermarket. Having watched TV every day during my childhood, she no longer wants to watch it. "TV is really dumb."

For the first time, she speaks of her life in the future tense: "In ten years, when he [her boyfriend] has stopped working, we'll buy an RV and live all over France—we'll travel. I've always dreamed of a life of travel."

A final memory. A few months ago, in the garden of a teahouse where I'd suggested we meet, she told me how she had once been called to the school by my teacher when I was six years old. The teacher wanted to tell her—at least this is what she claimed—that she, the teacher, found my behavior different from that of the other children, that I spoke of dreams and desires that were too grandiose, ambitions that were abnormal for children my age. She said that the others wanted to become firemen or policemen, but I spoke of becoming the king or the president of the republic; that I swore that as soon as I grew up, I'd take my mother far away from my father and that I'd buy her a château.

I would like for this book—this story of her—to be, in some way, the home in which she might take refuge.